CONTENTS

INTRODUCTION

People are visiting gardens open to the public in ever increasing numbers and one often hears the comment, 'Why don't we have a rock garden like that?' Judging by some of the 'plum puddings' that can be seen, that would appear to be easier said than done. Yet with some helpful guidelines to follow, it takes no more effort or expense to create a well constructed rock garden than one consisting of a pile of soil with rocks strewn about in a haphazard way.

Do not be put off by the scale of operations in botanical gardens and those large estates that were set out many years ago when financial support was easily forthcoming. A rock garden does not have to be large; in fact a distinct advantage in this kind of gardening is that an interesting collection of plants can be easily established in a very small space.

It is the intention in writing this guide that the practical advice offered will enable anyone to create a worthwhile project that will give continuous pleasure, not only to the gardener, but also to others who delight in enjoying plants.

The alpine house at Merrist Wood. Alpines can be grown under glass or outdoors.

1 • THE SITE

Few people are fortunate to have a natural rock garden, and so more often than not, it is a case of starting from scratch. Like the majority of plants that are cultivated, those used in rock gardens must be given suitable conditions so that they will grow properly.

Imagine the natural habitat of alpine plants, where they are free from winter damp and comparatively warm under the thick layer of snow in winter. In late spring and summer when the snow melts, they are bathed in the clear air and bright sunshine of the alpine slopes. The roots have sufficient moisture without being waterlogged, or in the case of moisture-retentive soil perhaps edging a stream, it is those plants that benefit from such conditions that we find growing there. In the garden situation, not only the true alpines as known by the botanist fit into the scene very nicely; other plants do as well.

Site

Choose the site for your rock garden with care – alpines in their natural surroundings enjoy an open prospect with plenty of light and clean, fresh air. Avoid an area that is overshadowed by trees: not only do the drips from branches in wet or foggy weather cause rotting in the plants below, but the tree's roots starve the soil of nutrients and moisture. Where trees are unavoidably present to the north and west, they should preferably be at least 45ft (14m) from the rock garden; those to the south and east should be even further away.

Common name Broom
Botanical name *Genista lydia* (syn *G. spathulata*)
Hardiness rating Hardy
Care rating Easy
Description Shrub with yellow flowers on green stems
Peak interest Summer
Height 2ft (60cm)
Spread 6ft (1.8m)
Growth rate Medium
Life span Several years
Uses Valuable for edges and ledges
Planting position Full sun
Soil needs Well-drained, acid soil
Propagation Take cuttings with a heel in late summer
Treatment Do not feed or mulch with organic material
Pruning Thin out old wood, lightly trim after flowering
Problems Shy to regenerate from old wood

A Paved Garden
(a) Slabs 12in (30cm) or more wide need to be used, otherwise the area will take on a patchwork effect. Rock in assorted size is best for the job, but keep it all the same kind to imitate a natural pavement. (b) Leave gaps no more than 1in (25mm) between some of the paving slabs. Fill the gaps with sandy loam and plant up with suitable subjects like trailing plants.

The ideal site for a rock garden is one that has a slight south or south-westerly slope and which is free from shadow and over-hanging trees that would drip on to plants below and invade the soil with their roots. The soil should be well drained and the site sheltered from wind. It should not be too difficult to provide these essential re-quirements in the majority of gardens, except that of freedom from shadow when it is cast by the dwelling house, or some other essential building. To be realistic, the majority of people these days who are interested in making a rock garden have a comparatively small area and it is a case of making the best of what is available. Indeed, rock plants can create more interest in a small garden than most other subjects, and that because of their size – a large number can be planted in a relatively small space.

Great care and a lot of thought need to be taken before construction begins: it is not the sort of job that can be started and completed in a weekend and then transferred to another place the following weekend after you have second thoughts. Get to know the garden and its peculiarities, for example, wind eddies around corners and through alleys, the frost pockets and where morning sun during winter may damage certain plants. Consider the proposed rock garden in relation to the remaining area and look at it from different angles.

The movement of water adds an interest-ing feature to a rock garden. Tumbling over rocks and into a stream or circulating by

A water feature adds interest to the rock garden.

Paved areas are maintenance free and provide the opportunity to sit out.

Cobbles inserted at various places add interest to a modern location. The stones need to be bedded into a mixture of one part cement to four parts builders' sand to avoid sinkage.

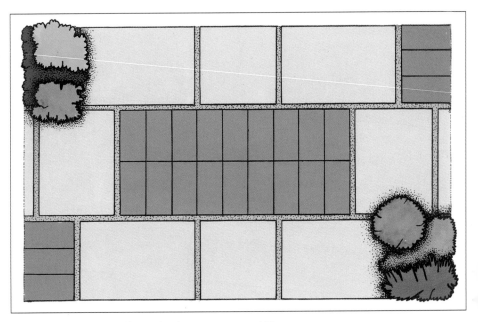

House brick or pavers can be used in the same way as cobbles.

Making a Miniature Rock Garden – Stage 1

An old porcelain sink can be turned into a miniature rock garden and, covered with home-made hypertufa, will look like a stone container. First cut away the waste pipe, leaving the strainer in place; then paint over the area to be treated with a suitable adhesive and allow to dry until tacky. The hypertufa mix of one part cement, three parts sand and one part fine peat by volume is made into a stiff, dryish paste and pressed on to the container's sides in small handfuls.

Making a Miniature Rock Garden – Stage 2

When the hypertufa has set perfectly hard after a few days, place 2–3in (50–75mm) of rubble over the base for drainage, cover the rubble with roughage from cocofibre and top up with medium. John Innes potting compost No. 2 mixed with a quarter of its volume of coarse sand is suitable for most plants; alternatively, use John Innes (acid) compost for those plants which require an acid root run.

Making a Miniature Rock Garden – Stage 3

Place one or two rocks in the surface and set out choice plants like dwarf juniper, lewisia and saxifrage. Mulch the surface with coarse gravel and water the plants well to finish off.

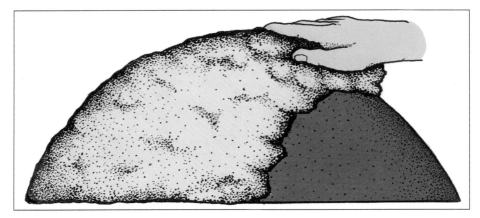

Containers of all shapes and sizes, including sinks, can be made from hypertufa. Make a mould from a heap of moist, compacted sand and press the small lumps of hypertufa together to form the desired shape. Dome shapes are structurally strong and the container can be made even stronger by inserting galvanised wire netting whilst the hypertufa is being applied. When the mixture begins to set, cut small drainage holes in the base.

Common name   Wall rue, spleenwort
Botanical name   *Asplenium ruta-muraria*
Hardiness rating   Hardy
Care rating   Easy
Description   Evergreen fern
Peak interest   All year round
Height   2in (50mm)
Spread   4in (10cm)
Growth rate   Slow
Life span   Perennial
Uses   Good for general planting, especially in crevices
Planting position   Shade
Soil needs   Moisture-retentive loam with good drainage
Propagation   Divide in spring or sow spores in summer
Treatment   Remove fading fronds
Pruning   Remove spent fronds
Problems   None

Making Moulds

With a little ingenuity, all sorts of household utensils can be brought into service, including buckets – one small bucket inserted into a larger one and rested on a bed of hypertufa makes a very desirable mould. If the smaller bucket is flimsy, it will need to be filled with compressed soil to keep its shape when the hypertufa is pressed between the two containers. Remember to cater for drainage holes: bottle corks or sawn off broom handle pieces are ideal and can easily be knocked out when the hypertufa has set.

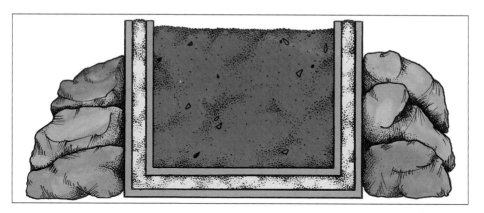

Cardboard boxes may be used in the same way as buckets; the larger box being supported at the sides with rocks and the inner box with compressed soil. Rip away the cardboard after a few days when the hypertufa is perfectly hard.

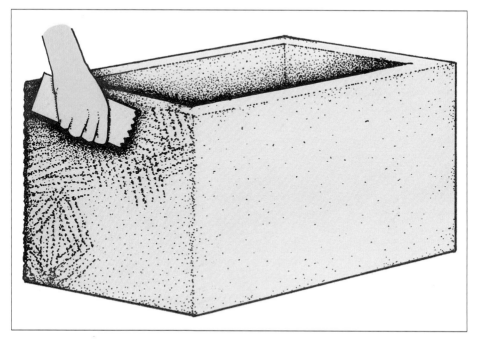

Containers made in smooth-sided moulds often need to be worked if they are to resemble old stone vessels. This is best done using a piece of flat wood to smooth the sharp edges, while a flat piece of boxwood with teeth cut into the working edge makes a very useful 'comb' to roughen the sides.

Sink gardens make good miniature rock gardens; they can be raised if necessary, to avoid stooping.

Some subjects are ideal for walls.

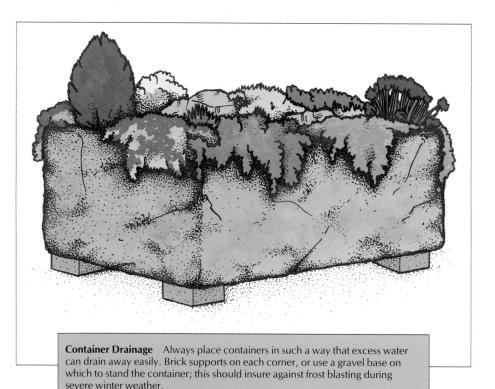

Container Drainage Always place containers in such a way that excess water can drain away easily. Brick supports on each corner, or use a gravel base on which to stand the container; this should insure against frost blasting during severe winter weather.

means of a pump, it will give endless pleasure, and small pools can be constructed in the rock garden so that the water trickles from one to another and back again. It is even better if water can pass below a surface that is topped with rock to form a moraine, or strewn with chippings to create a scree.

Once constructed, paved areas are much less time-consuming and laborious in terms of maintenance than a similar sized lawn area might be. Irregular crazy paving or flag stones can look very attractive, especially when plants are grown in the crevices with their roots in the cool, moist soil below and their shoots in the sun above. Other worthwhile features to consider include cobbles and setts, or bricks laid in interesting designs. The area need not be very large; in fact even a path can be made to look that much more attractive when paved and planted with suitable subjects. Quite often, attractive self-set seedlings find their way into such areas.

Sink gardens, stone troughs and other containers blend in well with paving, especially when plants are grown around the base of the container, and large rounded stones and water-worn rock also look attractive in such places. In fact, for those without a suitably large area to make a larger rock garden, very attractive miniature rock gardens can be made to accommodate plants in various containers. Raised beds provide another opportunity to grow plants, not only on the top, but also in the side walls.

2 • CONSTRUCTION

Before the actual practical work is attempted, it is worth designing the rock garden project on paper. Squared graph paper is best so that the dimensions can be scaled more easily. Try drawing from different angles so that you have the top, front, rear and side elevations to scale. This will help to finalize the plan because, no doubt, different ideas will present themselves as the drawings progress.

It is a good idea to make a list of requirements once the plans have been drawn up and an estimate of cost is also useful before work starts. This will ensure that sufficient funds are available to complete the project on time. It is worthwhile comparing prices from a variety of suppliers in order to get the best deal possible.

Materials

Transporting rock is a costly business and if a local quarry can be used, so much the better. Natural tufa is particularly expensive to purchase in quantity, although its bubbly perforations and indentations are ideal for accommodating small plants. Sandstone is inclined to be rather soft and prone to frost damage but it is very attractive and comparatively light – it has twice the volume of a similar weight of limestone. Limestone is used extensively in rock gardens while granite is not so popular now because of the high cost of haulage due to its density. It is also very hard and does not absorb moisture and so plants are not encouraged to cling to its surface. Which ever kind of rock is chosen, try to keep to the one type.

Use the same kind of stone throughout the project. Different sized stone, some very large and touching others to make ledges for the plants will help to make the rock garden look natural.

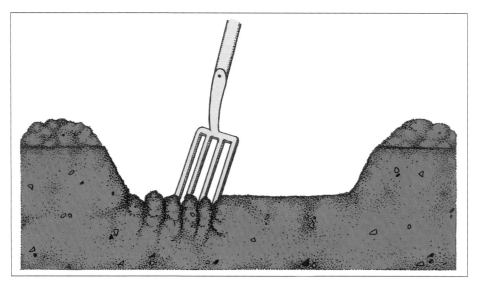

Poor drainage can be the result of a hard subsoil 'pan' caused by a layer of compacted soil or rock. If this is the case, dig down and break up the pan with a digging fork or crow bar. Otherwise a drainage system will need to be installed.

Chippings help to retain moisture below, at the same time giving good surface drainage.

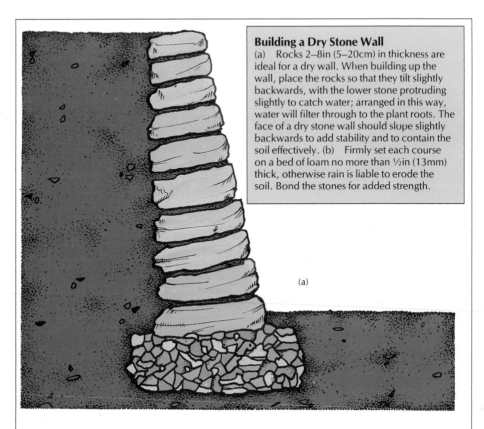

Building a Dry Stone Wall
(a)   Rocks 2–8in (5–20cm) in thickness are ideal for a dry wall. When building up the wall, place the rocks so that they tilt slightly backwards, with the lower stone protruding slightly to catch water; arranged in this way, water will filter through to the plant roots. The face of a dry stone wall should slope slightly backwards to add stability and to contain the soil effectively. (b)   Firmly set each course on a bed of loam no more than ½in (13mm) thick, otherwise rain is liable to erode the soil. Bond the stones for added strength.

(a)

(b)

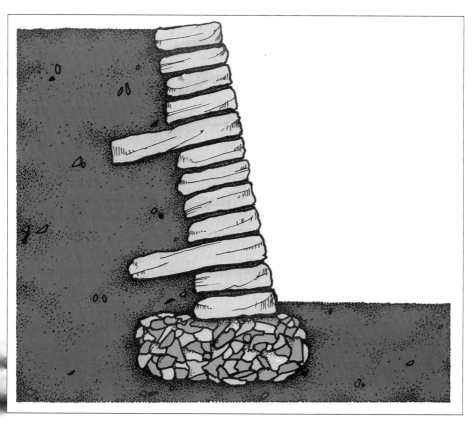

Dry walls over 3ft (90cm) high must be tied for added strength. Set long rocks so that the face is flush with the front of the wall and the 'tail' in the bank of soil. Stagger the ties 18in (45cm) one above the other and 6ft (1.8m) apart along the length of the wall.

Land drains may be necessary if the soil is not naturally well drained. They are available in lengths of slitted plastic tube as well as the traditional fired clay. Whether drains are required or not, aggregate may be necessary for base drainage, gravel to top it and chippings for the scree surface. Sand makes a good bed for crazy paving and slabs. Slabs can sometimes be obtained from the local authority and most garden centres have a selection of natural and reconstructed stone. Paving can be set on blobs of mortar instead of sand – if this is the case, cement will be required to mix with sand.

Cement is also needed to make mortar for walls, unless, of course, a dry wall is planned. Pools and water courses can also be formed by moulding cement, although butyl rubber is often used since it is frost-proof and will last for many years even when exposed to the sun – unlike PVC sheeting which must not be exposed.

Top soil, sand and cocofibre will be

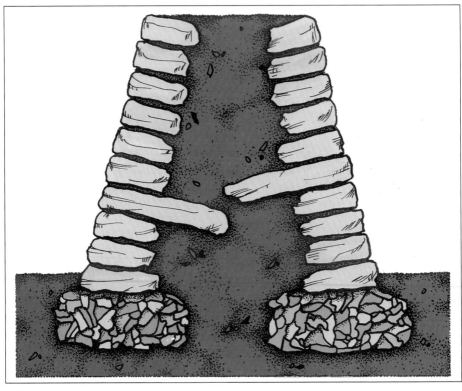

Build a double wall in a similar way to a single retaining wall, the only difference being that soil is infilled and rammed between the walls as they are built up. This method can also be used to construct a raised bed.

required for crevices and other planting areas. (Do not use peat as it is rapidly becoming a depleted resource.) The soil should ideally be a good loam, free from weeds and with a pH of 6.5 or thereabouts which is suitable for the majority of plants. Lime-free sharp sand is better than some builders' sand which tends to be rather fine and alkaline. Cocofibre is processed from coconut husks and is ideal for absorbing moisture while retaining air at the same time.

Purchased plants usually have a name label attached, although this may sometimes be flimsy and printed out by computer. This type tends to fade and unless a separate record is kept, the plant name may be lost or forgotten. White plastic labels with the plant name written in wax pencil are effective and do not stand out offensively on the scree, and in the case of a darker background, small metal labels painted black can be used with the plant name scratched out with a sharp, pointed instrument.

A cold frame is a useful item to bring on young plants and for propagation; pots, half pots and seed trays with pressers to fit each size are also required if propagation is to be undertaken. Polycarbonate sheeting cut up into smaller squares and supported o

Common name Thrift
Botanical name *Armeria juniperifolia*
Hardiness rating Hardy
Care rating Easy
Description Perennial producing dense tufts and pink flowers
Peak interest Summer
Height 2in (5cm)
Spread 6in (15cm)
Growth rate Fast
Life span Perennial
Uses Good for edging, scree, moraine and in small garden
Planting position Full sun
Soil needs Ordinary, well-drained soil
Propagation Cuttings in summer, division in spring, sow seeds in spring
Treatment Dead head
Pruning Remove faded flower heads
Problems Possibly rust in spring

Common name None
Botanical name *Juniperus communis* 'Compressa'
Hardiness rating Hardy
Care rating Easy
Description Dwarf conifer with slender columnar habit
Peak interest All year round
Height 2ft (60cm)
Spread 6in (15cm)
Growth rate Slow
Life span Many years
Uses A specimen plant on a raised bed
Planting position Full sun or partial shade
Soil needs Any ordinary, well-drained soil
Propagation Take cuttings with a heel in autumn
Treatment Needs shelter from cold winds
Pruning None required
Problems Scale insects, caterpillars, rust

galvanized wire is useful for protecting plants from winter damp and rain. Twin-walled sheeting is ideal for the job so that the wire can be threaded through the gap for support; the material is very tough, unlike glass which is often used to cover plants.

Soft, bubbly tufa is a natural lightweight rock.

Tools

A range of hand tools will also be needed. These include: dibber, trowels and hand forks for planting; spade, digging fork and rake for cultivation; and small swan-neck 'onion' hoe for weed control. A short length of broom handle is useful for ramming soil around rocks, and similar stakes and string will be necessary to mark out the site, although a flexible garden hose may be used instead. Although not absolutely necessary, a shovel is more useful than a spade for moving soil and for mixing mortar or compost. Other handy items include a long measuring tape and a spirit level.

A builders' trowel will be needed if rock or slabs are to be laid with mortar. Cutting tools for rock include a bolster (which consists of a wide blade chisel), a narrow bladed chisel and a 'lump' hammer. Purpose-made rammers are available for consolidating paved area foundations, or a

Common name   None
Botanical name   *Cotoneaster dammeri radicans*
Hardiness rating   Hardy
Care rating   Easy
Description   Prostrate evergreen shrub with red berries
Peak interest   Summer and autumn
Height   6in (15cm)
Spread   6ft (1.8m)
Growth rate   Fast
Life span   Many years
Uses   Attractive when growing over rock, scree, moraine and a sink
Planting position   Full sun
Soil needs   Ordinary with good drainage
Propagation   Remove self-layered stems, heel cuttings or sow seed in autumn
Treatment   Remove vertical shoots if they appear
Pruning   Cut back in early spring to keep within bounds
Problems   Aphids, scale insects, birds, fireblight

As an alternative to setting plants, seed can be sown in crevices.

heavy sledge hammer could be used. You may need a crow bar to move large pieces of rock; a wheelbarrow would certainly facilitate the removal of rocks, soil and various other items, and a bucket would also be useful. Finally, a watering can with fine and coarse roses will be needed for watering the plants.

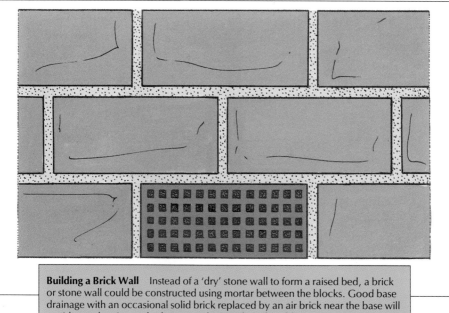

Building a Brick Wall   Instead of a 'dry' stone wall to form a raised bed, a brick or stone wall could be constructed using mortar between the blocks. Good base drainage with an occasional solid brick replaced by an air brick near the base will avoid waterlogging and subsequent damage from frost blasting in winter.

Planting in a Wall   Larger subjects are easier to plant as the wall is being built. Allow sufficient space around the plant for stem development and spread out the roots of bare-root raised plants to encourage quick establishment. Always set the plant at the base of a vertical joint.

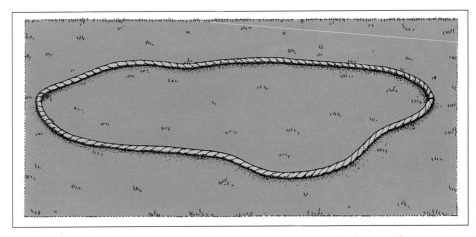

Mark out the rock garden site with rope or a flexible water hose, and stand back to view the area from distant vantage points – the outline should be as variable as possible. Bear in mind that in nature a few rocks are usually scattered here and there in front of the main alpine plant area, and where space permits the same should apply in the garden.

Method

Drainage is unlikely to be a problem on sloping ground, but where drainage is impeded on a more level site, dig out the soil to some 2½ft (75cm) and place an 8in (20cm) depth of stone rejects or aggregate in the bottom. Next spread a thin layer of shingle over the surface. Provision should be made to allow the water to flow away, either into a soakaway or by some other method. Now fill the excavated area with soil, firming it by treading with your heels as backfilling progresses. Drainage work provides the opportunity to remove any weeds, otherwise they must be removed before construction takes place.

It is worth remembering at this stage that in addition to the aesthetic appearance of the rock, its main functions are to retain soil and to keep roots cool and moist. Bearing this in mind, the rocks should be set so that they dip slightly backwards into the face of the rock garden in order to direct the moisture towards the plants. Bury at least one third of the rock into the ground on a very firm base, then use a rammer to pack the soil around the rock. Avoid a 'plum pudding' effect with many small rocks placed haphazardly. The strata of each piece of rock must be in the same plane, sloping slightly, and unless a moraine is being constructed, try to place each rock close to its neighbour with only a small crevice filled with rammed

Soil Drainage – Stage 1
Good drainage is essential for the well-being of the plants, since the roots are unable to function properly in soil that lies wet and airless for any length of time. An existing sloping site will reduce the amount of preparation necessary to create the right conditions. When poor natural drainage is suspected, dig a test hole 2ft (60cm) deep and fill with water. If the water is still there the following day, you will have to consider providing some form of drainage, otherwise the plants will not thrive.

Soil Drainage – Stage 2
Once the site has been marked out, remove the good topsoil and make a heap away from the work area. Then, take out the subsoil and keep it separate from the more fertile topsoil. A total soil depth of approximately 2 ½ft (75cm) should now have been removed. Place an 8in (20cm) layer of stone 'rejects' at the base of the hole for drainage – place the larger stones at the bottom, with smaller sizes graduating to the top. This will provide good drainage, provided that the water can escape naturally from the area, otherwise a soakaway will need to be dug.

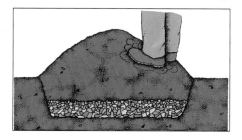

Soil Drainage – Stage 3
Return the subsoil, unless it is heavy clay, to the excavated area, treading it firmly as backfilling progresses. Finish with the topsoil so that the mound is at least 3ft (1m) high.

At least one third of the height of the rock should be below soil level for stability and it must be placed on a base made very firm by treading or ramming. Each rock should be well bedded against its neighbour by ramming soil around it. A good test is to stand on the rock when it is in position.

Placing the Rocks Try to avoid a 'plum pudding' effect when placing the rocks. The rock is there to retain soil and, to a certain extent, soil moisture in the root zone. Terraced rock looks good but a considerable amount of material is required. Quarried pieces with flat surfaces fit together well and better resist the erosion caused by heavy rain. Fill gaps with soil and small stones. Keep the rock grain (strata) pointing in the same direction with each piece.

Creating a Moraine – Stage 1

Some choice alpine plants thrive in the poorest of media; in fact, any hint of richness in the soil will encourage leaves rather than flowers. Those plants require moraine-like conditions that can be provided by constructing a gradually sloping bank of well-drained soil.

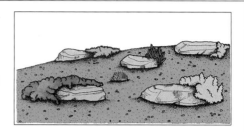

Creating a Moraine – Stage 2

Remove the topsoil and then the subsoil so that a total depth of 2ft (60cm) has been dug out. Spread a depth of 3in (75mm) of coarse stones over the base of the depression, then a 2in (50mm) layer of gravel. Over that, spread 6in (15cm) of fibrous topsoil, then complete with a mixture of five parts stone chippings (limestone chippings for those plants that require alkaline conditions), and one part by volume each sharp sand, cocofibre, loam and decomposed leaf mould. Remember that plants of the moraine really must have good drainage.

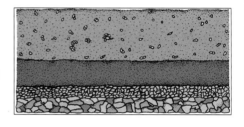

soil, making sure all the time that no air pockets have been left. Small wedges of rock with the pointed end placed uppermost in the crevice will help to bind the construction together. Large areas of the rock garden will be devoid of rock: it is a mistake to try to cover most of the ground, but the rock that is used should be placed with careful consideration.

Construct terraces as the work proceeds. Each terrace should vary in width and height from the one above and below, but do keep the slope in each individual terrace even and let an occasional terrace blend into another by adjusting its gradient. Soil erosion is likely to occur at steep gradients, so keep the slope at an angle less than 1:4. Rocks can be kept apart from those below by placing small stones in the fissure between, again making sure that the soil is rammed in well. Good topsoil can be brought in to form the mound on top of the feature, or a small valley could be constructed instead, but do avoid a dip that would retain water

unless you intend to make a water feature.

The plants will need to be tended from time to time, so it is an advantage to set large rocks at intervals to act as stepping-stones. Pathways of steps can be made to look natural and effective, and it goes without saying that they must be constructed on a sound foundation.

Large flat rocks varying in size and shape can be put in position to form steps. Design the path so that it is curved, rather than straight which is really too formal. Take care to ensure that the soil below is really firm.

Paving slabs could be used instead of rocks. Once the path area has been marked out, dig out the soil to a depth of 6in (15cm) and ram the base firm. Then half-fill the trench with hard-core or stone rejects and ram hard; a 2in (50mm) depth of shingle followed by 1in (25mm) of sand will bring the foundations to the surface. Rake level and lay the slabs, tapping them in with the handle of a heavy hammer.

3 • PLANT PROPAGATION

There can be fewer jobs more satisfying than creating new plants from old, whether it be from cuttings, division, layering, seed or from other means. Gaining experience by trying new methods is exciting and no amount of trial and error will exhaust the number of different kinds of plants that one can experiment on in various ways. One of the most stimulating accomplishments in gardening is to see roots on a young plant that was a rootless cutting a short while before.

Soft Stem Cuttings

Moisture retention with good drainage in a mixture free from pests and diseases are the requirements of a good rooting medium – John Innes seed compost meets the requirements for the majority of cuttings. Very small specimens may do better if the surface is topped off with sharp or silver sand, and it is encouraging to see that gardeners are returning to the use of coconut fibre to replace peat.

Soft stem cuttings are taken at a time when the plant is in active, healthy growth. The length of stem removed depends on the size of the parent plant, bearing in mind that within reason a large cutting will take less time to make a comparatively large plant than a small one. The cutting should be taken from the parent complete with growing point but without flowers or flower bud – the cambium cells from which roots emerge are most active just below the leaf joint and so the stem of the cutting should be cut through with a sharp blade at this point. Stems with internodes of ½in (13mm) or more can be snapped cleanly from the parent and inserted into the rooting medium without further trimming, provided there is no snag of skin that is likely to rot back.

The active ingredients in rooting 'hormone' powder encourage root·initiation and the product also contains a fungicide to

Soft stem cuttings are taken from the non-flowering green tips of shoots. Cut them with a sharp blade, just below a leaf joint and insert them into rooting medium as soon as possible after removing them from the parent plant.

control any diseases that may be present. It is therefore worthwhile dipping the base of the cutting into the powder before tapping off the surplus and inserting the stem into the rooting medium. A liquid formulation is also available, but do dilute the concentrate exactly according to manufacturer's instructions, otherwise the result may be similar to a hormone weedkiller.

Remove one or two lower leaves from the cutting so that none remain either below the level of the medium or touching it after insertion (soft cuttings normally should not be inserted any deeper than is necessary to support them vertically). Insert the cutting by pushing it carefully into the medium and space it so that it does not touch its neighbour, then give the container a good watering with a fine rose on the end of a watering can. Once the container has drained, place it in a propagating case or frame shaded from strong sunlight. Alternatively, the container may be put into a polythene bag to

Common name   Crane's bill
Botanical name   *Erodium reichardii*
Hardiness rating   Hardy
Care rating   Easy
Description   Densely tufted plant, pink-veined, white flowers
Peak interest   Summer
Height   3in (75mm)
Spread   9in (23cm)
Growth rate   Fairly slow
Life span   Perennial
Uses   Plant on ledges, wall and moraine
Planting position   Full sun
Soil needs   Moist, sandy soil with good drainage, pH7
Propagation   Seed, stem or root cuttings
Treatment   Deep, well-drained soil, sun, winter protection
Pruning   None
Problems   Generally trouble-free, but aphid can be a problem

Common name   Violet
Botanical name   *Viola stojanowii*
Hardiness rating   Hardy
Care rating   Easy
Description   Rhizome producing an evergreen plant with yellow flowers
Peak interest   Late spring to summer
Height   3in (75mm)
Spread   3in (75mm)
Growth rate   Fast
Life span   Perennial
Uses   Attractive edging plant for the small garden
Planting position   Full sun
Soil needs   Good drainage
Propagation   Sow ripe seed or take soft cuttings in summer
Treatment   None
Pruning   Dead head to prolong flowering season
Problems   Leaf rot, pansy sickness, rust

retain moisture so that the cuttings do not shrivel, and the application of gentle bottom heat at 61°F (16°C) will encourage faster rooting. Enthusiasts fortunate enough to have a mist propagating bench with heating cables below the containers will find that the cuttings root in 10–14 days, otherwise they may take another week or so.

When roots have formed, gradually wean off the cuttings by reducing the humidity. After a few days they will be ready to pot off or line out in the frame.

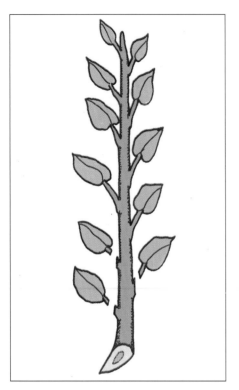

Semi-ripe (also known as half-ripe) cuttings are usually taken during the summer, when the base of the non-flowering stem has become firm.

Semi-Ripe Cuttings

During summer the base of a plant's stem becomes firm, and this is often a good time to take cuttings from plants which do not produce roots readily from soft growth. The cutting can be prepared in the same way as for soft stem cuttings, except that the stem will no doubt need to be cut rather than snapped from the parent. Cuttings with a 'heel' often root more easily than otherwise. A heel is a sliver of tough stem retained when the shoot is pulled downwards to remove it from the parent; there is often a small strip of rind attached to the base of the heel and this should be trimmed away before insertion.

Common name   Creeping juniper
Botanical name   *Juniperus procumbens* 'Nana'
Hardiness rating   Hardy
Care rating   Easy
Description   A compact, spreading conifer with dense growth
Peak interest   All year round
Height   1 ft (30cm)
Spread   3 ft (1m)
Growth rate   Slow
Life span   Many years
Uses   Good for ground cover
Planting position   Full sun or partial shade
Soil needs   Any ordinary, well-drained soil
Propagation   Take cuttings with a heel in autumn
Treatment   Prune to keep within bounds
Pruning   None required
Problems   Scale insects, caterpillars, rust disease

Common name   Kidney vetch, ladies'
fingers
Botanical name   *Anthyllis montana*
Hardiness rating   Hardy
Care rating   Easy
Description   Mat-forming, deciduous shrub
with pink flowers
Peak interest   Late spring to autumn
Height   6in (15cm)
Spread   6in (15cm)
Growth rate   Medium
Life span   Perennial
Uses   Ground cover and to plant on rock
ledges
Planting position   Full sun
Soil needs   Loam with good drainage
Propagation   Cuttings with a heel in late
summer or by seed
Treatment   Dead head
Pruning   None required
Problems   None

Common name   None
Botanical name   *Aubrieta deltoidea*
Hardiness rating   Hardy
Care rating   Easy
Description   Compact evergreen trailer,
flowers red to purple
Peak interest   Spring
Height   4in (10cm)
Spread   2ft (60cm)
Growth rate   Fast
Life span   Perennial
Uses   Good for edging, moraine, carpet,
walls and paving
Planting position   Full sun
Soil needs   Well-drained, ordinary soil,
preferably with some lime
Propagation   Cuttings in spring or division
in late summer, sow seeds in spring
Treatment   Dead head trailers
Pruning   Cut back after flowering to tidy
up
Problems   White blister, downy mildew

Hardwood Cuttings

Shrubs and other plants that produce woody stems can be propagated by removing mature shoots in late autumn. Hardwood cuttings are usually longer than other kinds and can be taken with or without a heel. The more hardy plants can be propagated in a sheltered spot out of doors in well drained soil. A cold frame can be used for all subjects, with the cuttings inserted directly into the base or into containers. Hardwood cuttings take several months to

Common name None
Botanical name *Haberlea rhodopensis*
Hardiness rating Hardy
Care rating Challenging
Description Rosette plant; blue/lilac flowers with a yellow throat
Peak interest Spring
Height 4in (10cm)
Spread 8in (20cm)
Growth rate Fairly fast
Life span Perennial
Uses Attractive in crevices, good for small garden
Planting position North-facing in shade
Soil needs Well-drained soil with added leaf mould
Propagation Leaf cuttings or division in spring
Treatment Protect from winter rain
Pruning Remove spent flower heads
Problems Prolonged wetness rots rosettes, slugs

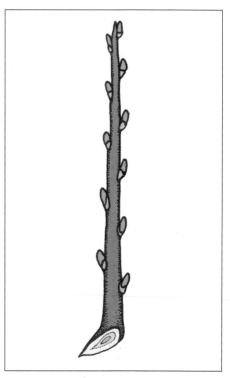

Hardwood cuttings are taken from deciduous plants any time after the leaves have fallen – from the end of October up to the end of the year. They are best pulled gently from the plant so that a small 'heel' of wood from the main stem stays attached. Trim the tip of the heel back to the wood but not into it.

produce roots large enough for the young plants to be lined out or planted in their final position.

Leaf Cuttings

Plants with fleshy leaves can often be propagated by removing a leaf from the parent and inserting it into rooting medium. The best method is to remove a leaf that is almost fully grown together with its stalk.

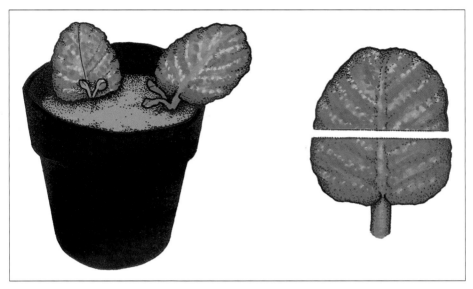

Leaf cuttings will root when taken from certain plants, especially those forming rosette type growth. Remove the leaf together with its stalk by pulling downwards. Place the leaf cutting on to the surface of a mixture of cocofibre and sharp sand, with the leaf stalk firmly embedded in the medium.

Reduce the length of the stalk by half, insert it into a well drained rooting medium and place it in a room or greenhouse with a temperature of 65–70°F (18–21°C). Keep the container shaded from bright sunlight and it will produce roots and plantlets from the leaf stalk. Small, fleshy, stalkless leaves can be laid flat on the surface of the medium while large leaves are often cut through at the widest part and inserted vertically.

Root Cuttings

Plants with fleshy roots can be propagated by digging them up in late autumn or early spring and removing some of the roots. Those the diameter of a pencil are ideal and should be cut into lengths from 2–6in (5–15cm) in length. Cut the end closest to the crown of the parent straight across and cut the base through at an angle so that there can be no confusion as to which end is which when it comes to inserting the cuttings.

A shady situation in well-drained soil out of doors, or a cold frame is suitable for the root cuttings which should be inserted with the slanted end pointing downwards so that the top of the cutting is approximately 1in (25mm) below the surface of the medium. Instead of inserting vertically those plants that produce horizontal roots just below the soil surface, they should have their root cuttings inserted horizontally at the same depth as when they were attached to the parent.

Keep the rooting medium moist but not too wet, and the cuttings should produce roots and shoots during the summer following insertion. They can then be transplanted

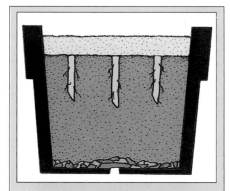

Root Cuttings

Root cuttings can be taken from plants with fleshy roots, but the parent plants will need to be lifted and it may take them some time to re-establish themselves. Roots which are approximately the same diameter as a pencil are ideal and should be cut into lengths of ¾–1in (18–25mm) in length. Cut the base with a slanting cut so that you know which way to insert the cutting. Insert the cutting into a mixture of cocofibre and sharp sand with the top of the cutting just above the surface; then, sprinkle sharp sand to a depth of 1in (25mm) on top of the rooting medium.

to their final position the following autumn or spring.

Runners

Some plants produce plantlets on the end of stems while others produce stems that root at the node. These two types are the easiest plants to propagate because you simply need to sever the stem between offspring and parent. The plantlet may or may not have roots at this stage. If it has roots it can be transplanted straight away, if not it will need to be encouraged to form roots by placing it on to a moisture-retentive but well-drained medium, and at this stage it may be necessary to peg down the plantlet

Common name   Pasque flower
Botanical name   *Pulsatilla vulgaris*
Hardiness rating   Hardy
Care rating   Easy
Description   Long stems with violet flowers, fluffy seed heads
Peak interest   Spring
Height   9in (23cm)
Spread   12in (30cm)
Growth rate   Fast
Life span   Perennial
Uses   Moraine, especially close to dark-leaved plants or dark rock
Planting position   Sun or partial shade
Soil needs   Light soil with good drainage; chalk is an advantage
Propagation   Sow fresh seed in summer or take root cuttings in summer
Treatment   Needs well-drained soil
Pruning   None
Problems   Grows rather lush in heavy soil

by its severed stem with a piece of bent wire.

Certain plants produce offsets around

their crown; these are really plantlets on miniature runners and can be treated in the same way.

Division

Crown-producing plants can be divided by lifting the clump with a digging or hand fork depending on the size of plant. Young crowns on the edge of the clump are preferable and are teased away with the fingers, taking care to keep the roots intact. Larger clumps can be divided by inserting two forks back to back and pulling the main clump apart. On no account should a spade be used to cut the clump into pieces, as the cut surfaces may not heal before infection gains entry. Discard the old crowns in the centre of the clump and plant up the healthy young portions as soon as possible. Late summer to early autumn is the best time to divide those plants that flower in spring and early summer, while spring is the ideal time to divide plants that produce flowers in the autumn.

Layering

Plants that are difficult to propagate can often be encouraged to form roots by bending a stem downwards and pegging it below soil level. Subjects with tough or woody stems are prepared by exposing the cambium with a slanting cut just below a node, upwards into the stem. The wound is then secured just below soil level with a bent

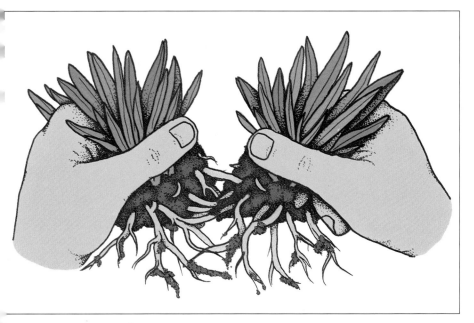

Fibrous rooted plants that produce crowns can be increased by division, although they may take a year or two to regain their attractive shape. Carefully lift the plant with a hand fork and shake as much soil as possible from the roots. The crowns can then be teased apart with the fingers and replanted as soon as possible into their new quarters.

wire, and the free end of the shoot tied vertically to a stake. This ensures that the cut portion remains open with as much of the cambium as possible exposed to the soil.

Inspect the layered shoot after a few months and when new roots have formed, sever the new plant by cutting through the stem on the parent side, and then transplant it to its final position.

Seed

Seed may take a few weeks or a few months to germinate, and although plants raised from seed usually take longer to mature and

Common name   Common polypody
Botanical name   *Polypodium vulgare*
Hardiness rating   Hardy
Care rating   Easy
Description   Evergreen fern
Peak interest   All year round
Height   12in (30cm)
Spread   Under 12in (30cm)
Growth rate   Fast
Life span   Perennial
Uses   General planting, especially in crevices or walls
Planting position   Sheltered shade
Soil needs   Dry, sandy soil enriched with leaf mould is ideal
Propagation   Divide in spring or sow spores in summer
Treatment   Plant rhizomes on surface and peg down with wire
Pruning   Remove faded fronds
Problems   Rust

Common name   Saxifrage
Botanical name   *Saxifraga grisebachii*
Hardiness rating   Hardy
Care rating   Easy
Description   Cushion plant with red, star-shaped flowers
Peak interest   Spring
Height   4in (10cm)
Spread   6in (15cm)
Growth rate   Fast
Life span   Perennial
Uses   Excellent for the small garden, moraine and containers
Planting position   Sun
Soil needs   Well-drained, gritty loam, pH7 or alkaline
Propagation   Division best, seed may produce inferior plants
Treatment   Mulch with grit around stem base
Pruning   Remove spent flower stems
Problems   None

flower compared with those propagated vegetatively, it is a method to be commended when a large number of plants need to be acquired at low cost; in any case, some plants are difficult to propagate by other means. It is also a way of distributing species amongst enthusiasts.

Common name   Gentian
Botanical name   *Gentiana verna*
Hardiness rating   Hardy
Care rating   Challenging
Description   Tufted perennial producing deep blue flowers
Peak interest   Late spring and summer
Height   4in (10cm)
Spread   6in (15cm)
Growth rate   Fast
Life span   Two to three years
Uses   Ideal for edging, ledges and moraine in small gardens
Planting position   Full sun – south-east facing is ideal
Soil needs   Well-drained, fibrous loam, pH7
Propagation   Containers of sown seed out of doors in winter, or division
Treatment   Keep roots moist in spring and summer
Pruning   None
Problems   Short-lived unless protected from winter rain

Generally speaking, it is better to sow seed as soon as it is ripe or within a year of harvesting, although certain species produce seed that is viable for a longer period. This depends on the storage conditions – unopened vacuum-packed seed will still be viable after a long period.

Saving and Storing Seed

Many enthusiasts save seed from their own plants with success. It should be borne in mind that hybrid plants do not usually produce offspring identical to themselves, and there is a chance that the flowers of the seed-bearing plant may have been cross-pollinated by another variety, so that the resulting seedlings may produce variable plants. Do not be too hasty to gather seed until the seed heads have matured properly. On the other hand, if the seed head has ripened fully the seed may have been dispersed naturally from the capsule before it is harvested.

To harvest the seed, remove it from its receptacle and then dry it, preferably on a sheet of paper in the sun for a few days, protecting it from birds. The seed can then either be sown straight away, or stored in greaseproof paper bags in a cool, even temperature and kept dry and dark. If there is any doubt about the dryness of the atmosphere, store the seed in tightly closed tins or dark bottles. The dry seed may also be placed in polythene bags and stored in the refrigerator.

Sowing Seed

John Innes seed compost is suitable for the majority of rock garden plants. Properly mixed with the correct ingredients it provides good drainage and sufficient nutrients for the seedlings until they are pricked out. Half pots that are used by commercial growers for dwarf pot chrysanthemums make useful containers for seed sowing;

Sowing Small Seed Sow very small seed by sprinkling it evenly and spacing it out well on the surface. A piece of folded paper facilitates sowing, then just press the seed into the surface of the medium. With larger seeds, cover no more than twice their diameter with medium.

they are sufficiently shallow to make extra drainage in the form of the traditional layer of crocks in the base unnecessary when proper John Innes seed compost is used. The medium tends to be warmer if plastic pots are used and requires watering less often because moisture is not evaporated from the wall of the container. The medium is likely to stay wet longer, however, if it is overwatered and especially if a poorly drained mixture has been used. Clay pots evaporate moisture through the wall of the container, and the medium tends to be cooler and slightly less likely to remain too wet for too long. In all cases, watering should always be carried out with care.

Tap the container on a hard surface once or twice after filling with compost to just below the rim, and then press the surface lightly with a flat object to make quite sure that the surface is level. Large seed can be sown straight on to the medium and covered by up to twice its own diameter of similar medium. Small seed should be sown on to a fine bed of sand sifted over the surface; the seed can then simply be pressed into the sand, or covered very lightly with sand passed through a fine sieve. Sow small seed thinly and evenly to encourage sturdy seedlings that are less likely to damp off. Inexperienced gardeners may find it helpful in this respect to mix the seed with dry sand and sprinkle the mixture

Common name None
Botanical name *Primula juliae*
Hardiness rating Hardy
Care rating Easy
Description Bright purple-red flowers on top of long stems
Peak interest Spring
Height 4in (10cm)
Spread 12in (30cm)
Growth rate Fairly fast
Life span Two to three years
Uses Edges and crevices in small moraine
Planting position Semi-shade
Soil needs Ordinary well-drained soil with leaf mould added
Propagation Sow fresh seed in summer
Treatment Remove dead leaves before they rot
Pruning None
Problems Aphid, caterpillar, vine weevil, crown and foot rot

Common name Pyrenean primrose
Botanical name *Ramonda myconi* (syn *R. pyrenaica*)
Hardiness rating Hardy
Care rating Easy
Description Stemless herbaceous perennial with deep pink flowers
Peak interest Late spring/summer
Height 4in (10cm)
Spread 9in (23cm)
Growth rate Fairly fast
Life span Perennial
Uses Ideal for north-facing crevices in small gardens
Planting position Shade or semi-shade, preferably vertical
Soil needs Good drainage, enriched with leaf mould
Propagation Sow seed, divide in spring, or leaf cuttings in summer
Treatment Water during dry periods to avoid scorch
Pruning None
Problems Will not tolerate strong sun

over the surface, omitting the sand bed that would otherwise have been provided.

On no account should the seed be watered in after sowing. Any moisture that is required should be provided by immersing the container in a vessel of water so that the moisture seeps in without disturbing the seed. Allow the container to drain and place it in a cold frame or propagator – place a sheet of glass or PVC on the container so that the medium retains moisture, and a sheet of paper on top of the glass to exclude light. The glass (or PVC) should be turned daily to disperse the condensation.

Remove the paper and glass when the seedlings emerge (this can be up to several months after sowing with some species). It will be necessary to shade the tender seedlings from strong sunlight during the day and when water is required, immerse the container in a vessel of clean water for a few minutes until moisture can be seen at the surface, then remove the container and allow to drain.

Pricking Out

The seedlings should be transferred to another container as soon as they can be handled without damage – ideally at the seed leaf stage. Hold the seedling by a seed leaf rather than by its stem which is more easily bruised. John Innes potting compost No. 1 is satisfactory for most plants and the size of container used depends on the number of plants of that sort to be pricked out. Use a dibber to make a hole which is large enough to accommodate the roots without them buckling. After inserting the seedling so that the cotyledons are just above the surface of the medium, press the dibber lightly into the medium at the side of, but not touching, the stem. Shade the young plants for a few days to let them establish.

Prick out seedlings as soon as they can be handled: small plants yet to produce their first true leaf establish much faster than larger seedlings. It is important to hold them by their seed leaves rather than by the stem or true leaves as these will bruise easily.

Having pricked out the batch of seedlings that have germinated, more seeds may germinate, and so it is advisable to replace the seed container in the propagating area – it is sometimes the case that the slower seeds to germinate produce the best plants.

Hardening Off

When the risk of frost is past and the plants are large enough, they can be hardened off by gradually giving them more ventilation. They may then be either potted off, or planted out into their final position in the garden.

Open-Ground Sowing

Although this is possible for some of the more vigorous kinds, it is not usually prudent to sow rock garden plants in the open ground. However, when this method is the only course open, thorough preparation of the seed bed (which should be shaded and sheltered from drying winds) is necessary. A well-drained but moisture-retentive, light soil is required. Avoid working the soil if it is too wet – a good time to do this is when the surface can dry off within an hour of raking. Rake the surface to a fine tilth and make sure that it is firm and level without dips or bumps: the finer the seed, the finer the surface crumbs should be. Allow the soil to stand for a few days so that weed seeds germinate – it is far easier to deal with as many of them as you can before sowing than after the cultivated plants have germinated.

Once the soil has warmed up (a good indication of this is when weed seeds begin to germinate in the spring), sow the seed thinly in drills approximately 6in (15cm) apart. The depth of drill will depend on the size of seed: large seed will require a drill ½–1in (13–25mm) deep; medium-sized seed needs a drill up to ½in (13mm) deep; and fine seed barely requires any covering

at all. Apart from very fine seed that is finely covered with sand, seed in drills can be covered with the soil that was taken out to make the drill. Lightly firm the soil after sowing with the rake head.

An ideal soil moisture content exists

Common name   Mountain avens
Botanical name   *Dryas octopetala*
Hardiness rating   Hardy
Care rating   Easy
Description   Evergreen mat-forming sub-shrub with white flowers
Peak interest   Summer to Autumn
Height   4in (10cm)
Spread   2ft (60cm)
Growth rate   Seedlings flower in three years
Life span   Perennial
Uses   Attractive when sprawling over rock
Planting position   Full sun
Soil needs   Moisture-retentive loam, good drainage, pH7
Propagation   Lift rooted stems, cuttings in summer, seed
Treatment   Protect from cold wind
Pruning   Remove spent flower stems
Problems   Transplanting difficult, resents root disturbance

When propagating from seed, ensure that the pots are labelled and sheltered.

when a handful of soil can be squeezed in the palm of the hand and no excess moisture oozes out but the ball remains intact when the hand is opened. During very dry weather, the bottom of the drill can be covered with a layer of sifted cocofibre and watered with a can. After the seed has been sown, the seed bed may be watered with a fine rose on the end of the can.

Take precautions against birds by running strands of black cotton between sticks over the seed bed. Slugs and other pests may take a liking to the seedlings as they germinate – *see* page 54 for information on how to deal with this problem.

Keep the seed bed free from weeds and thin out the surplus seedlings as soon as they can be handled – this will help to encourage sturdy growth in those that are kept. The seedlings that are to be grown on should be transplanted before they compete with each other, otherwise they will become spindly and drawn.

Make sure that each different kind of seed sown has a waterproof label so that the plants can be identified at a later date. It is a good plan to keep a diary of sowing dates and a simple sketch to mark the position of

Common name   None
Botanical name   *Chamaecyparis obtusa* 'Nana Compacta'
Hardiness rating   Slightly tender
Care rating   Easy
Description   Dome-shaped conifer with bright foliage
Peak interest   All year round
Height   2ft (60cm)
Spread   2ft (60cm)
Growth rate   Slow
Life span   Many years
Uses   Attractive planted by rock
Planting position   Full sun or partial shade
Soil needs   Any ordinary well-drained soil
Propagation   Take cuttings with a heel in spring
Treatment   Requires shelter from cold winds
Pruning   None required
Problems   Subject to wind damage

each kind is worthwhile, just in case a label goes missing.

4 • CULTIVATION

Newly constructed rock gardens should be left for two to three weeks to settle completely. The soil should be moist but not too wet for planting and on no account must planting be carried out when the soil is frozen. Make sure that the rootball of the plant is moist before transplanting, especially when the plant is being moved on from a container.

When to Plant

Early autumn is a good time to plant bare root subjects in areas without too severe a climate; the plants will then have a good chance to settle in and develop a sound root system before summer. In cold districts it is better to wait until spring before planting, taking care to ensure that the roots do not suffer from the effects of spring wind and dry weather in early summer. Plants growing in containers can be planted at any time as long as the soil is not too wet or frozen.

Method

With a trowel, make a hole that is larger than the roots which are to be accommodated – the roots will then be given sufficient space without being crushed or damaged. Plant firmly, spreading out the roots of bare root plants and water well afterwards. Stone chippings placed over the soil around the plant will help to retain soil moisture and at the same time provide a localized area of drainage around the neck.

Take care when planting in a crevice that there is no air pocket at the base to dry out the roots. Such areas should be filled with a gritty, loamy potting compost for those subjects like *Adonis* and *Androsace* that benefit from this kind of treatment. *Alyssum* and *Aubretia* also grow well in crevices. Bear in

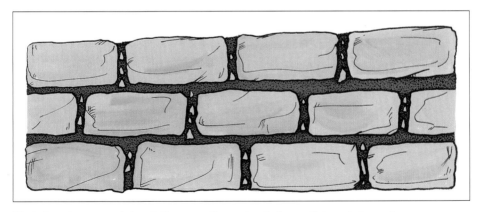

Vertical crevices are made in a similar way to fissures by placing small stones between the rocks; in some cases it is prudent to place several small rock pieces in larger gaps all surrounded by rammed soil to help avoid erosion during winter frost and rain. When wedge-shaped stones are used, keep the wide edge pointing downwards so that any settlement of soil can easily be topped up. Vary the gradient when constructing terraces; too steep and rain will erode the soil, too level and the soil may stay too wet. A gradient of up to one in four should fit most requirements. The height and width should also vary to make a more interesting subject. Construct the terraces so that they blend into one another from time to time.

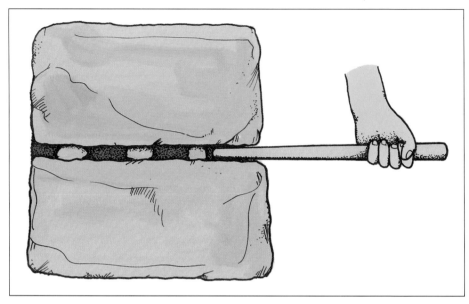

Rocks placed one on top of the other are held apart by placing small stones between them. The gaps are then filled by ramming in soil to make fissures to accommodate plants. Make sure that the lower rock projects slightly beyond the one above, so that water collects to irrigate the plants growing in the fissure. Air pockets should be avoided, otherwise roots will not be able to establish properly.

Leave areas of soil between your outcrops of rock with just the occasional single rock in place here and there. It is likely to be a far more effective project when a larger area is covered by the rock garden with the material available, rather than cramming it all into a smaller site.

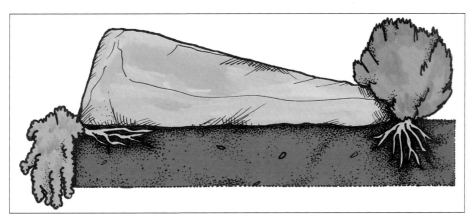

Make sure that the face of each rock is in line with the soil beneath, so that the piece does not overhang and restrict water from reaching the roots of plants below. The rocks are placed so that their rears slope backwards, thereby directing rain-water to the root area of the plant.

On all but very small rock gardens, flat stones are placed at convenient stations to facilitate tending the plants and for stepping around the feature to remove weeds.

Paving slabs can be made from large pieces of rock by splitting through the strata seams with a bolster.

mind the requirements of other plants like shade lovers such as *Cyclamen* and *Ramondia,* sun lovers like *Erodium* and *Geranium,* and the saxifrages which will cover the larger rocks and lower areas.

Maintenance

One year's seeding means seven years' weeding, so remove weeds by hand or as a last resort with the aid of an onion hoe before they have a chance to establish; a mulch of chippings will do much to suppress the growth of weed seedlings.

Plants that are susceptible to damp will need protection from autumn through the winter and into spring. This is best achieved by placing a sheet of polycarbonate or glass supported by galvanized wire legs over the

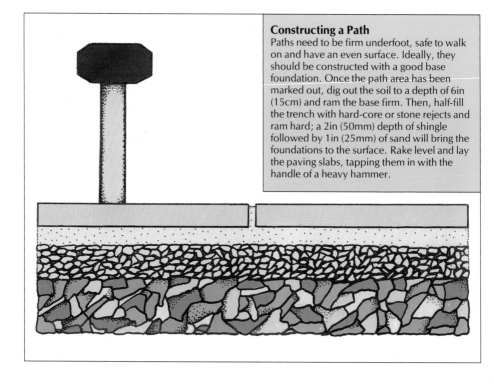

Constructing a Path
Paths need to be firm underfoot, safe to walk on and have an even surface. Ideally, they should be constructed with a good base foundation. Once the path area has been marked out, dig out the soil to a depth of 6in (15cm) and ram the base firm. Then, half-fill the trench with hard-core or stone rejects and ram hard; a 2in (50mm) depth of shingle followed by 1in (25mm) of sand will bring the foundations to the surface. Rake level and lay the paving slabs, tapping them in with the handle of a heavy hammer.

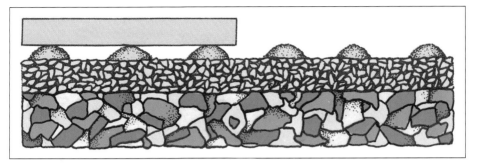

Omit the sand and bed the paving slabs on blobs of mortar if the path is likely to be used a great deal.

plant. Delicate little plants that require further protection may be provided with walls of the same material, with a gap in each side for ventilation

During early spring plants will benefit from a top dressing mulch consisting of a mixture of equal parts by volume of loam, grit and cocofibre. The top dressing will help to retain soil moisture, but do check the soil from time to time during the summer and irrigate as necessary. A watering can fitted with a rose will suffice for small

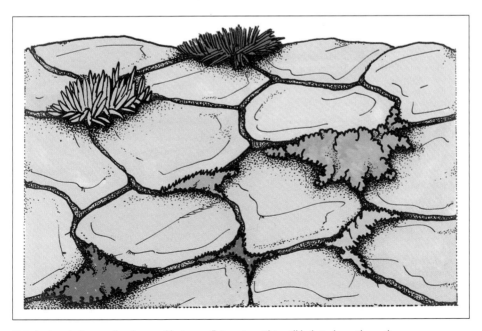

Set plants out along path edges and between flat paving. This will help to keep the path informal and combine it with the whole.

Constructing Steps

(a)   Steps must be very firm to avoid rocking. Use the largest rock that you can obtain to add greater stability and to accommodate feet comfortably when walking. Lay the slabs on rammed soil, or concrete them in for safety. The rise between steps should be at a convenient height – normally 6in (15cm) or less. Lay each step so that it overhangs the rise by 1in (25mm).

(b)   Lay slabs one on top of the other for steps with a gradual incline or use deeper rocks as risers. Remember that the step should overhang the rise by 1in (25mm).

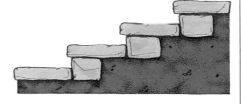

(c)   Leave gaps of 2–3in (50–75mm) between the slabs to accommodate plants. Fill the gaps with a good, well-drained loam such as correctly made John Innes potting compost No. 1.

(d)   Prepare the foundations in the same way as for a path (*see* the keynote on page 44) and make sure that the site has good drainage. Tap the slabs into the sand, checking all the time with a spirit level; a length of straight timber can be used with the spirit level to check a large area.

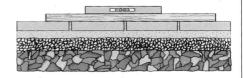

Large flat rocks varying in size and shape can be put in position to form steps – design your path so that it is curved, rather than straight which is really too formal. Take care to ensure that the soil below is really firm.

areas, while larger rock gardens will need an overhead sprinkler to apply sufficient water during dry periods. When irrigation is applied, it should always be sufficient to moisten the top 3–4in (7·5–10cm) of soil at least; a trickle just sufficient to moisten the surface will do more harm than good by encouraging the roots to come to the surface.

Ageing New Rock
Ageing the appearance of newly quarried or reconstructed rock with an application of boiled rice water, or the traditional 'cow tea' – cow pats mixed with water. That encourages the growth of algae and moss and so should not be applied where accidents are likely to occur on the resulting slippery surfaces.

Planting Scheme Unless the rock garden is very small, a better effect will be achieved by planting groups of three or more of the same kind of plant. This will avoid giving a fragmented appearance to the scheme and hasten a mature look. Avoid planting rampant trailers close together and take care to set the plants so that the top of the rootball is level with the soil surface.

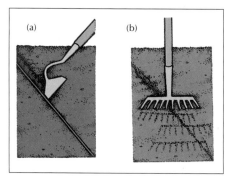

(a) Prepare a shallow trench for planting using a garden line and hoe. (b) After planting, level the soil with the back of a rake.

Unless seed is to be saved, remove spent flower stems as soon as the flowers fade so that the area will retain a well kept look; allowing unwanted seed heads to develop wastes the plant's energy that could otherwise be utilized in developing growth. Plants that grow beyond bounds and encroach upon others may be pruned by trimming back after flowering.

Whether to feed the plants or not rather depends on the type of soil in which they are growing: a sandy soil tends to lose soluble plant food quickly, whereas a heavier type, particularly one containing a certain amount of clay, will retain the major plant foods over a long period. In any case,

The roots of some plants are prone to rot in any but the most acutely drained media. In light, sandy soil all that may be required is the addition of crushed gravel dug into the top spit. Those plants that require even better drainage can be accommodated at planting time with the addition of extra grit in the root zone.

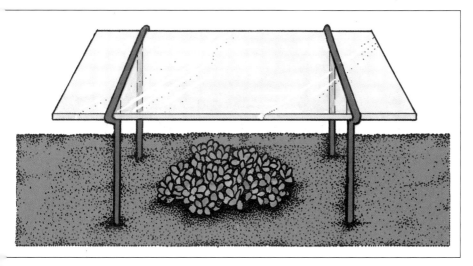

Certain plants, especially those with hairy leaves that retain moisture, need protecting from winter rain. A sheet of glass or rigid, transparent plastic suspended over the plant from late autumn to spring will help to ward off rot brought on by dampness.

Surface Crusts   Some soils are subject to capping with a hard surface crust, especially when sun follows heavy rain, and in this state the soil is unable to breathe and the plant roots are liable to suffocate. Whilst the only long-term remedy is to improve the soil structure by correcting surface drainage and incorporating bulky organic material like cocofibre, the surface cap should be crumbled in the meantime with a small hand cultivator.

Remove dead flowers with their stems as soon as the flowers fade. The exception to the rule is when seed is to be saved, and in the case of plants that develop attractive seed heads, they may be retained to extend the interest of the plant.

Mulching Mature plants spread their leaves and stems over the soil surface and provide a soil-moisture-retentive mulch, but until the plants have become established, a mulch of stone chippings will serve the same purpose. Mulching will help to avoid a soil surface cap and will also prevent weed seedlings from becoming established.

nitrogen and some trace elements are brought down from the atmosphere in rain. Many rock garden plants have the ability to delve well down into the soil to search for food; their need for fertilizer is not so great as compared with vigorously growing plants and so on balance it is better not to apply supplementary fertilizer to plants that are growing in an open rock garden. Exceptions would be for those plants growing in small containers and in this case, proprietary compounds applied according to the manufacturer's instructions may be used.

Mains water is rather alkaline in some areas and can cause nutritional problems by 'locking up' certain elements like magnesium, iron and manganese; plants that are sensitive to pH levels are then better provided with collected rain water, or deionized water. Foliar feeding with a soluble fertilizer containing trace elements can often cure plants that are deficient of those nutrients.

5 • PESTS AND DISEASES

Gardening is a challenge! Unfortunately slugs and other pests appreciate our plants just as much as we do, and although rock garden specimens do not attract invaders any more than other kinds, it is prudent to be ever watchful and to take remedial action as soon as you can.

In many cases it is possible to steer clear of trouble, and prevention is always better than cure. Provide the correct environment for a plant so that it grows properly, and it will stand a far better chance of resisting disease infection. As far as fauna is concerned, we need to consider the balance of nature; for example, to kill all the birds that tear our favourite plants to shreds would mean that we would be inundated with armies of insects. Respect and common sense combined with a little guidance is often the answer so that nature works with us, and much can be done by keeping a garden tidy and free from rubbish and weeds.

Ants

Ants have the annoying habit of burrowing around roots, thus causing plants to wilt. They also make their nests below ground, often tunnelling below rocks, and aphids are encouraged by these pests who like to 'milk' them for honeydew. Early spring is a good time to tackle ants as this is when the colony is particularly active with its new offspring. Empty tins smeared on the inside with honey or treacle will soon swarm with the pests and these can then be submerged in boiling water. Absorbent material such as a rag or sponge can be soaked in a syrup of sugar water to attract ants and then doused with boiling water to kill them.

Common name   Creeping Jenny, moneywort
Botanical name   *Lysimachia nummularia* 'Aurea'
Hardiness rating   Hardy
Care rating   Easy
Description   Bright yellow stems, leaves and flowers
Peak interest   Summer
Height   4in (10cm)
Spread   12in (30cm)
Growth rate   Fast
Life span   Perennial
Uses   A good carpet plant for ground cover
Planting position   Sun or partial shade
Soil needs   Moisture-retentive or dry soil
Propagation   Division or cuttings in autumn or spring
Treatment   Likes moisture
Pruning   None
Problems   None

Birds

Birds sometimes peck buds and petals, especially during spring; sometimes they are looking for insects but more often than not they are simply being mischievous. Mirrors, cotton thread draped around the plants, reflective strips that glitter in the breeze, 'humming twine' that makes a high pitched noise in the wind and plastic bottles with flaps cut in the sides that are suspended upside-down on a stake have all been tried with varying levels of success.

Caterpillars

Caterpillars can soon defoliate plants but are easy enough to pick from the leaves by hand. Look closely over the plants at every opportunity and squash the eggs before they have a chance to hatch.

Cats

Whilst efficient in catching mice and frightening birds, cats themselves can be a nuisance. They dislike the smell of orange peel and naphthalene and so it is worth placing either of these around the rock garden, especially where the cat enters.

Damping Off

Damping off of hairy leaved plants can be a problem during late autumn through to spring. Water collects on the leaves and softens the tissue, thereby creating ideal conditions for fungal diseases to gain entry. A sheet of glass or polycarbonate suspended over the plant will do much to keep the rain off until spring when the leaves will dry off faster under more favourable weather conditions. A surface mulch of stone chippings around the base of a plant will help to prevent stem rot. Attention to soil drainage is, of course, most important. It may be necessary to use a fungicide, or replace disease infected soil as a last resort. Some diseases are waterborne so keep storage vessels clean and well covered to omit airborne spores.

Earwigs

These insects feed on the flowers of some plants. They can be caught by laying down traps made by stuffing straw or newspaper into a flower pot, rolling crumpled paper into a ball, or rolling corrugated paper into a tube and holding it with an elastic band. The contents of these traps should be inspected during daytime. A hollow portion of plant stem or a bamboo cane, or a potato cut in half with the contents scooped out and turned upside-down on the soil also make good hideaways which attract earwigs.

Froghoppers

Froghoppers secrete a froth, hence their other common name of cuckoo-spit. The insects suck sap from the plant but are easily removed by spraying forcibly with clear water.

Honey-Fungus

This is a disease that attacks the root system of many plants. It spreads through the soil by means of black strands that resemble long shoelaces, hence its other common name of bootlace fungus. A white mycelium can be seen when the bark of woody plants is peeled back just above soil level. Any plants infected should be removed and disposed of together with the soil.

Leatherjackets

These are the dirty brown, legless larvae of crane flies which prove troublesome when they feed on roots or nibble at stems. They are particularly prevalent in weedy ground and can be controlled by regular hoeing since they reside near the soil surface.

Naphthalene forked into the soil at the rate of 2oz per sq yd (68g per sq m) followed by a thorough watering should control the pest.

Rodents

Mice can be troublesome, especially during cold weather when they feed on bulbs, corms and seed. A mouse trap baited with a small piece of chocolate or a large seed does the trick.

Rabbits are very destructive in some rural areas where they can soon reduce a number of plants to ground level. Garden twine dipped in fox oil and suspended a few inches above the ground around the rock garden makes a good deterrent.

Rust

Rust disease causes brown pustules to form, usually on the undersurface of the leaf, while smuts develop black, dusty spores. These diseases soon reduce the vigour of the plant and affected leaves should be removed as soon as they are seen.

Scale Insects

These insects are like minature tortoises and attack plants that have a tough rind or bark. They reduce vigour by sucking sap from their host, and secrete a sticky honey-dew that attracts sooty mould and wasps. The bark can be scraped and then washed forcibly with a jet of clear water to rid the pest, or the scales can be dabbed with methylated spirit.

Slugs and Snails

Slinky slugs and snails that do their damage at night by eating holes in leaves and stems

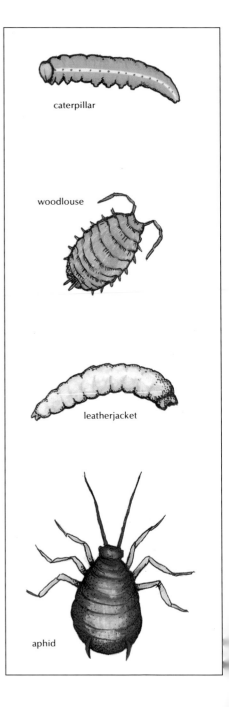

caterpillar

woodlouse

leatherjacket

aphid

can be disposed of by hunting them down in the dark with a torch. Another method that has stood the test of time is to create a barrier. Cut zinc sheeting into strips 1½in (38mm) wide, bend the strips into a ring and join the ends with copper wire, then place each ring around a plant so that it encircles it completely without the leaves protruding over the top. It may be that sufficient electricity is generated by the interaction of zinc and copper to give the creatures a slight shock, or perhaps they simply do not like the sensation of metal on the skin!

Other means of dealing with the problem include traps of various kinds that can be put down on to the soil, close to the susceptible plants. Slugs and snails usually hide away from predators and the drying effects of the sun during daylight hours. Large cabbage leaves placed on the soil to form a dome, upturned grapefruit skins, and pieces of tile therefore make effective traps. Take the trapped pests far enough away into the country so that they are unable to find their way back, or sprinkle them with salt. Jars sunk into the ground and filled with beer lure no end of slugs, but there is always the chance that beneficial beetles may also be caught. Frogs and toads have a healthy appetite for slugs and snails, and thrushes should also be encouraged for their liking of snails. The soil around calciphilous plants can be dusted thickly

Common name Whitlow grass
Botanical name *Draba rigida*
Hardiness rating Hardy
Care rating Easy
Description Densely tufted cushion plant with yellow flowers
Peak interest Spring
Height 1in (25mm)
Spread 3in (75mm)
Growth rate Slow
Life span Perennial
Uses Plant with other dwarf specimens near porous rock
Planting position Full sun
Soil needs Sandy with good drainage
Propagation Sow seed during spring, or division in late summer
Treatment Winter rain protection, keep moist at other times
Pruning Remove flowers as soon as they fade
Problems Rosettes inclined to rot when watered from above

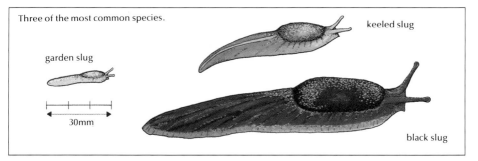

Three of the most common species.

keeled slug

garden slug

30mm

black slug

Slugs are a real problem for all gardeners.

Common name   Stonecrop
Botanical name   *Sedum spathulifolium*
Hardiness rating   Hardy
Care rating   Easy
Description   Evergreen plant with succulent, silvery leaves
Peak interest   Summer
Height   2in (50mm)
Spread   Over 9in (23cm)
Growth rate   Fast
Life span   Perennial
Uses   Good carpet plant for a crevice or dry site in a small garden
Planting position   Sun or semi-shade
Soil needs   Good drainage
Propagation   Division during spring or summer
Treatment   Needs sun
Pruning   None
Problems   None

with a dressing of hydrated lime to control the pests.

Vine-Weevil Larvae

These larvae feed on the roots of some plants and have a particular liking for primulas and cyclamen corms. Unfortunately the damage has already been done when the symptoms (wilting plants) are seen, and prevention here is better than cure. Adult weevils feed by night, eating serrated-edged holes in the leaf margin; during the day they usually hide away in crevices at the base of the plant.

Viruses

Viral diseases are often troublesome when sap-sucking insects are allowed to spread the infection from plant to plant. Viruses show in a number of different ways, including mottling of foliage, stunted growth and leaf spots encircled by rings. There is no cure once the plant has become infected and the disease will be present in any propagating material taken from the plant.

Wireworms

These are the larvae of click beetles and attack the underground parts of plants by burrowing into the flesh. Portions of carrot or potato buried just below the soil surface attract the pests which can be dealt with simply by removing them. Replace the bait every two or three days.

Woodlice

Woodlice normally feed on decomposing vegetable matter, including wood. However, they are very partial to seedlings and leaves that touch the ground. They shelter during the day in the same way as earwigs and can be controlled with the same methods.

Woolly Aphids

This insect exudes a waxy protective coat resembling cotton wool. It causes the same kind of damage as the scale insect and can be controlled with the same methods.

The weather in different locations, and even in the same place can vary considerably from year to year, and will have a bearing on when the actual operations are carried out. The following diary of events is therefore meant to be used as a guide only, and interpretation should be made with consideration to local conditions.

Early Spring

Frost and snow will still be lying on many gardens, so take care if construction work is being undertaken – slippery ground and rock, especially when handled by cold fingers can be dangerous. However, this is a good time to undertake construction projects and if the inclement weather deters working, take advantage of the time to go over plans and sketches to see if they need to be altered. A trip to see established rock gardens, or alpine houses is also always worthwhile.

Keep an eye on winter protection in the form of glass or polycarbonate sheets which cover susceptible plants. Without a protective covering of snow, some plants are inclined to dry out during frost and windy conditions. Firm soil around rocks and plant roots that have been loosened by frost – newly constructed rock gardens and plants set out recently are at particular risk from the effects of frost.

Check containers that were previously sown with seed to ensure that they are still protected against vermin and prick out any seedlings that are ready for moving on. Newly acquired seed should also be sown as soon as possible to achieve the best possible results.

Plants in flower at this time (depending on season and location) include:

Adonis amurensis, Anemone blanda, Cyclamen coum, C. vernum, Hepatica nobilis, Primula denticulata and *P. marginata.*

Common name	Sowbread
Botanical name	*Cyclamen hederifolium*
Hardiness rating	Hardy
Care rating	Easy
Description	White or pink flowers appear before leaves
Peak interest	Autumn
Height	4in (10cm)
Spread	6in (15cm)
Growth rate	Large corms flower in first year
Life span	Many years
Uses	Good for naturalizing
Planting position	Sun or partial shade, sheltered by rock or shrub
Soil needs	Well-drained loam with leafmould added
Propagation	Seed
Treatment	Plant corms just below soil surface
Pruning	None
Problems	None

Late Spring

Many plants will now start to take interest in the longer days and higher daytime temperature, including weeds. Remove weed seedlings as soon as they appear and before they have a chance to compete with the cultivated plants. Weeds may also attract pests such as aphids unless they are dealt with at an early stage, and slugs and snails can also be a problem at this time. Check plant labels and replace any that have been

lost or removed by birds. This is particularly important in pockets where bulbs were planted previously and have yet to show above the soil surface.

Construction work should be completed as soon as possible, so that planting up can start as soon as the soil warms a little and becomes congenial. Spread out the roots of bare-root plants when planting, plant firmly and water in well; place chippings around the neck of plants, especially those that are prone to neck rot.

Tidy up generally and remove old, spent leaves from herbaceous plants. Protective sheets of glass and polycarbonate should be taken away, cleaned and stored as weather improves and before the strong sun scorches leaves. Replenish surface mulch to areas that have worn thin. Apply fertilizer if required.

Many plants can now be propagated by division, including:

Achillea ageratifolia, A. kellereri, Androsace carnea, A. sarmentosa, Adiantum pedatum, Anemone blanda, Asperula gussoni, Asplenium adiantum-nigrum, A. fontanum, A. officinarum, A. ruta-muraria, A. septentrionale, A. trichomanes, A. viride, Blechnum penna marina, Campanula alpina, C. cochleariifolia, C. pulla, Crassula sarcocaulis, Cryptogramma crispa, Cystopteris alpina, C. bulbifera, C. fragilis, C. montana, Draba aizoides, Drosera rotundifolia, Edraianthus serpyllifolius, Erodium chrysanthum, E. amanum, E. petraeum, Gentiana verna, Geranium argentium, G. subcaulescens, Iberis sempervirens, Lewisia cotyledon hybrids, Meconopsis aculeata, M. puniceus, Mertensia pulchellum, Morisia monanthos, Oenothera pumila (and cuttings), *Onoclea sensibilis, Oxalis adenophylla, Phlox sub-*

Common name   Cobweb houseleek
Botanical name   *Sempervivum arachnoideum*
Hardiness rating   Hardy
Care rating   Easy
Description   Dense leaves form rosettes with cobweb-like hairs
Peak interest   Summer
Height   1in (25mm)
Spread   12in (30cm)
Growth rate   Fast
Life span   Perennial
Uses   Ideal for crevices or walls in small garden
Planting position   Sun or semi-shade
Soil needs   Light soil with good drainage
Propagation   Division; seed can produce inferior plants
Treatment   Needs sun
Pruning   None
Problems   None

ulata, Phyllitis scolopendrium, Physoplexis comosa, Pinguicula vulgaris, Polypodium calcareum, P. dryopteris, P. phegopteris, P. vulgare, Primula capitata, P. denticulata, P. farinosa, P. forrestii, P. fortunei, P. marginata, P. rosea, P. verticillata, P. viscosa, Ramondia myconi, Rhododendron intricatum (and cuttings), *Saxifraga* × *apiculata, S. boydii, S. burserana, S. bursiculata, S. diapensioides, S. grisebachii, S. longifolia, S. oppositifolia, S. retrusa, S. rocheliana, S.*

(Opposite)   Spring is colourful in the rock garden.

Summer colour in the rock garden.

salomonii, *S. sancta, S. scardica, S. stribrnyi, S. thessalica, Sedum pulchellum, Sempervivum arachnoideum, S. calcareum, Shortia uniflora, S. giganteum, Woodsia hyperborea, W. ilvensis,* layer *Daphne rupestris.*

Walk round to check soil firmness after frost and continue to check seed containers for germination. Sow seed as it is delivered. Cold frames, especially those used for propagation, may need shading as the sun gains strength.

Early Summer to Mid-Summer

Days are lengthening and as the soil warms up with the sun gaining strength, there is a chance that plants, especially those recently set out, may need supplementary irrigation during dry periods. Give the plants sufficient water to reach the lower depths rather than just a sprinkling of water that would evaporate quickly; watering during the evening is more effective than watering during the day.

Keep a look out for pests that attack the plants. Those above ground can usually be seen easily but those below – such as root aphids and the larvae of vine weevils – are often missed until the plant shows signs of distress. Cut off withered foliage from early flowering bulbs, and ensure that any holes in the soil above narcissus bulbs are filled in to deter egg-laying by the narcissus fly.

Collect seed when it is ripe and bag up to store in a cool, airy place until it is convenient to sow. It is time to:

layer *Dianthus alpinus;* take cuttings of *Dianthus pavonius, Edraianthus serpyllifolius, Erodium chrysanthum, E. amanum, E. petraeum, Phlox subulata, Sempervivum arachnoideum, S. calcareum* and *S. acaulis;* divide *Saxifraga × apiculata, S. boydii, S. burserana, S. bursiculata, S. diapensioides, S. grisebachii, S. longifolia, S. oppositifolia, S. retrusa, S. rocheliana, S. salomonii, S. sancta, S. scardica, S. stribrnyi* and *S. thessalica;* and sow seeds of *Dianthus pavonius* and *Silene acaulis.* Fern spores can be sown when they are ripe during mid-summer.

Some trailing plants that are becoming invasive can be cut back after flowering.

Late Summer to Early Autumn

Rock gardens in their first year of existence will be providing a great sense of satisfaction now: plants set out last autumn or spring should have established themselves and begun to make new growth. Make a note of any rearranging that may be necessary and take photographs to jog the memory when it comes to carrying out the work.

Keep on top of the weeds, preferably by hand weeding. Some pernicious deep-rooted weeds such as bindweed may only succumb to a hormone-type herbicide, but be very careful with application as even a speck touching a wanted plant inadvertently will probably kill it. Early autumn can

still produce bright sunshine and so do not be in too much of a hurry to remove shading from a greenhouse or cold frame. Roller blinds really come into their own at this time of the year, when the odd dull day can be followed by bright weather.

Plants that can be propagated by division in autumn include:

Achillea ageratifolia, A. kellereri, Adonis amurensis, Anemone blanda, A. hortensis, Arabis alpina, Campanula alpina, Campanula pulla, Campanula cochleariifolia, Hepatica nobilis, Mertensia pulchellum, Physoplexis comosa, Primula capitata, P. denticulata, P. edgeworthii and *Saxifraga* spp. Take cuttings in early autumn of *Androsace carnea, A. sarmentosa, Arabis alpina, Dryas octopetala, Edraianthus serpyllifolius, Geranium argenteum, G. subcaulescens, Nierembergia rivularis, Rhododendron intricatum* and *Silene acaulis.* Sow seed of *Campanula alpina, C. pulla, C. pusilla, Primula edgeworthii* and *Rhododendron intricatum,* and layer *Rhododendron intricatum.*

Late Autumn to Winter

Remove debris that blows on to the rock garden and lay traps for slugs. Secure a sheet of glass or rigid polycarbonate and cover susceptible plants to prevent water from lodging on those that have hairy leaves, and to protect cushion types and others that may be prone to rot.

Try to get construction work started whilst the weather is still reasonably congenial – bare root deciduous shrubs can be planted at any time during the dormant season, soil conditions permitting. Inclement weather provides the opportunity to catch up on many jobs – essential reading, cleaning containers, renewing plant labels, setting vermin traps in frames and ordering new and replacement plants and seeds.

GLOSSARY

Acid (soil) Having a pH below 7.
Aggregate A mixture of different sizes of stone.
Alkaline (soil) Having a pH above 7.
Apex The uppermost tip of a stem.

Bare root Roots that are not surrounded by a medium as in a container-grown plant.
Bolster A chisel with a flat blade for splitting rock and bricks.
Builders' trowel A flat-bladed hand tool for spreading mortar.
Bulky organic Material derived from living organisms; for example, cocofibre and animal manure.

Calciphilous A lime-loving plant.
Cambium Undifferentiated plant cells that give rise to roots, or form calloused over wounds and so on.
Compost A mixture of loam, sand and cocofibre or other ingredients to make a potting medium for plants.
Cotyledon The seed leaf of a plant.
Cutting A portion of root, stem or leaf of a plant used for propagation.

Dead head To remove the spent flower stems and unwanted seed heads from a plant.
Dibber A cylindrical tool usually made from wood or plastic which is used to make planting holes for seedlings.
Division A method of propagating plants by dividing the rootstock.
Dry wall A wall built without the use of mortar to hold the blocks together.

Evergreen A plant that retains its leaves for more than a year.

Fertilizer Chemical that provides plant food.

Harden off To acclimatize plants gradually to cooler conditions.
Hardwood cutting A portion of mature stem to be used for propagation.

Heel The small portion of old wood at the base of a stem cutting.
Hypertufa A mixture of cement, peat (cocofibre) and sand made to resemble tufa.

Internode The part of a stem between two leaf joints.

Layering A method of propagation by pegging a stem down to the soil.
Leach To remove soluble salts from the soil by the action of water.
Loam A friable, fertile soil.
Lump hammer A comparatively heavy, hand-held hammer.

Moraine A mass of debris originally carried by glaciers.
Mulch A surface layer of bulky organic or inorganic material, such as cocofibre or stone chippings, which is spread on top of the soil.

Node A leaf joint on the stem of a plant.

Offset A daughter plant or bulb growing from the base of the parent.
Onion hoe A small hand-held tool with a blade on the end of a handle for loosening the soil surface and killing weeds.

Pan (1) A crust on top of the soil caused by heavy rain, or a hard layer of soil or mineral below the surface.
Pan (2) A container used for plant propagation.
Paved area An area of ground that has been covered by slabs of rock or stone.
Peat Partially decomposed vegetation, usually acidic and varying in colour from pale yellow to black according to the source.
Perennial A plant that lives for three years or more.
pH A scale that measures acidity or alkalinity. pH7 is neutral, below pH7 is acid, above pH7 is alkaline.